THIS BOOK BELONGS TO

TEST COLOR PAGE

WRITE DOWN YOUR FAVORITE ASPECTS OF THIS BOOK

Thank you very much

for trusting and choosing our product

Wish you all the best in your future

Hope you will put your trust in our next product.

Printed in Great Britain
by Amazon

32577701R00059